W9-AXA-501

LET IT BE
easy

LET IT BE
easy

SIMPLE ACTIONS
TO CREATE AN
EXTRAORDINARY
LIFE

TOLLY BURKAN

Council Oak Books
San Francisco / Tulsa

Council Oak Books, LLC
Tulsa, OK 74104
www.counciloakbooks.com

First edition, first printing
Printed in the USA
Cover design by Buffy Terry
Interior design by Melanie Haage

LIBRARY OF CONGRESS CATALOGING-IN-PUBLICATION DATA

Burkan, Tolly.
Let it be easy : simple actions to create an extraordinary life /
Tolly Burkan.-- 1st ed.
p. cm.
ISBN 1-57178-180-3
1. Self-actualization (Psychology) I. Title.
BF637.S4B87 2005
158--dc22   2004026863

contents

Dedicated with love to the memory of
DEVA
my soul-mate for 30 years.
Sweetie, may you dance with peace and joy forever.

note from the author

I WOULD LIKE PEOPLE TO KNOW SOMETHING RIGHT UP front. I am one of the happiest people you will ever find. However, when I was in my twenties, I twice tried to kill myself. The fact that today, at 57, I am happy, well adjusted, and successful is actually quite remarkable. I'm a parent. I'm healthy. And I'm free of the overwhelming self-doubt that almost cost me my life.

This is no small thing. Going from someone hell-bent on suicide to the opposite end of the spectrum, to me, is miraculous.

My process of waking up was the result of insights that changed the way I was thinking. They are contained in this book. I did not want to write a book that was like any other book, because what I have to share is different than anything you've ever read. This book is a wake-up call.

Tolly Burkan
Twain Harte, California

acknowledgments

I would like to thank my brother Barry Burkan for the time he spent improving the initial manuscript. I also want to express my appreciation to all my teachers, past and present, who are too numerous to mention, but who all know the part they played in my own personal evolution.

introduction

WHETHER IT'S HEAVEN OR HELL, YOU CREATE your life. If you are constantly struggling with your finances, relationships, health and career, life is hell. Once you learn how to let everything flow and materialize with ease, life can be heaven.

By and large, most people find life to be a struggle. The reason for this is that they were never taught that life can be easy, and they were never taught how to bring about the ease, comfort, safety and peace that makes life a rich, rewarding and joyous experience.

In elementary school and high school, we learn to master

the sciences and arts. At home, we acquire tools for social interaction. College teaches us how to earn a living. Yet after consuming all this knowledge, why are so many of us unhappy as adults? Is it because we arrived in adulthood only to discover that something crucial was missing? We were never taught how to be happy, how to develop high self-esteem, and how to be masters of our own destinies.

Simple Ideas + Action = Powerful Change

Historically, we have been led to believe that anything of value must entail a struggle to be acquired. I myself spent decades operating within that universal paradigm. It had never occurred to me that I could simply let life be easy. Now, however, instead of efforting to *make* things happen, I have mastered the strategy of *letting* things happen. The result is that I am healthier, happier and more prosperous than I ever imagined possible. If your life seems stressful, unexciting or limited, it is an indication that something vital is missing and that you have allowed yourself to stop growing. *Let It Be Easy* provides a simple framework for examining yourself in a way that can reveal the missing ingredients. After reading this book, you will be able to finally take charge of your life in a way that will bring you everything you've ever wanted. You will also be able to identify and eliminate what you don't want. This promise may seem inflated, but be assured, many people are doing it right now.

The keys to this knowledge are available to anyone willing to look beyond the traditional realms of education and explore these simple, profound reminders to take action.

This book suggests actions you can take that will immediately enrich your life and produce an environment in which harmony and fulfillment can thrive. They are simple ideas that can create dramatic results. When you take these actions, you will find a remarkable difference in the quality of your life. They can transform your day-to-day experience of living.

Let it be easy!

They will contribute to your sense of well-being, they will improve your relationships with others, and will assist you in becoming more alive, successful and prosperous.

Sometimes we move so fast traveling through life that even though we sense something may be off, we never really know what it is. After completing this book, however, at any moment, you can stop, look within, and ask, "What is it that I should be doing right now?" If you pause long enough to ask the question, there will be an answer. The answer will be that you have overlooked one of the actions this book recommends.

The ideas in *Let It Be Easy* are so simple and straightforward, just knowing about them will improve your thinking in a way that will immediately create noticeable changes in your life. To maximize your full potential, designate today as the beginning of a new phase in your life — the phase where you commit to becoming a more conscious and more conscientious human being. Using this book as a starting point, this process can be easier than you would ever dare to imagine. But you have to take action. *Let It Be Easy* is built on eleven ideas. The first four are simple points to remember. Then come the seven ingredients of an extraordinary life. Together they offer eleven actions you can initiate if you wish to obtain the most out of living.

Take Action Now!

Write the words *Let It Be Easy!* on several small cards or slips of paper.

- Tape one on your bathroom mirror.

- Put another card on your refrigerator.

- Stick one on the dashboard of your car.

- Slip another card into your wallet.

- Place a reminder on your desk.

Notice over the span of the next few days, how you make things difficult by telling yourself certain activities are hard.

Think about how you can change that perception.

Re-mind yourself that compared to childbirth, this task is a piece of cake.

Maintain your mind change by consciously focusing on the cards each day. Let them re-"mind" you that you have the ability to experience things in a different mode than you have in the past.

Watch how resisting certain actions actually creates more stress than learning ways to harmonize.

Gradually, you will begin learning life's lessons from your own insights. Soon, you will automatically start choosing the paths of least resistance and life will become sooooo much easier.

Let it be easy.

Teach to learn

Life is meant to have challenges. The challenges help us grow and mature. Your state of "mind" can make any challenge either more challenging or less challenging . . . even easy.

If you wish to enjoy inner peace and outer effectiveness in the world, you must walk your talk. You have to be an example of what you believe. Everything about you must be congruent. Wherever you find a discrepancy or contradiction in the way you are conducting your life, allow it to be a red flag calling your attention to where you must work on yourself.

Don't beat yourself up for not being a model of perfection; just notice where you still have rough spots that require further polishing. In time, you will be smooth and shiny, just like a jewel. As you grow, you'll certainly notice that you are changing. You'll find that situations that used to make you go berserk, are now handled with dignity and aplomb. Other situations may still challenge you, and that's okay. Just like a flower unfolding, you are in a process of evolution. If you try to manually force a rose to open, you destroy it. View yourself in a similar fashion. I have found that the best way to learn a skill is by teaching it to others. As you go through the process of teaching,

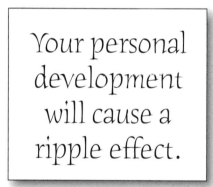

Your personal development will cause a ripple effect.

you are forced to assimilate the skill, and usually have to demonstrate it. The best teachers, teach by example. If you're a parent, parenting is an ideal opportunity for both teaching and personal growth. . . yours and your child's.

Many skills cannot be taught, but they can be caught. I have tried to teach my own children how to be a good friend by letting them witness how I treat my own friends. I assist my friends when they have needs — like driving a friend to an appointment when his car is in the shop for repairs. When my friends get sick, I'll often help take care of them by doing their shopping or cooking them a meal.

I teach my children generosity by letting them see how important it is in my own life. Not only am I generous with my children and my family, I encourage my children to be generous to others. When I make financial contributions to worthy causes, I let my kids in on what I am doing and why I am doing it.

Shine your light

As you grow in consciousness, as you become more effective in the world, as you witness your own personal development, your "light" will begin to shine. Not only is it okay for you to feel good about this, you are actually serving others by letting your light shine — right out there in public! Your peace, your confidence, your sense of well-being can be an inspiration for others. It's been said before: Don't hide your light under a bushel.

As you integrate *Let It Be Easy* into your life, people will notice the change in you. Rather than proselytize about what you are doing, let people witness your own transformation. Without trying, you become a teacher for others simply by your own example. People will start coming to you with open, sincere questions. You will be able to influence them more if you let them approach you, rather than you approaching them with an intention of changing them.

Your sincerity cannot help but impress your friends. As you grow, they will also be inspired to grow . . . because suddenly your words and actions are examples of the new you. Thus, your own personal development will cause the ripple effect, and in this way, you yourself are contributing to the overall improvement of the planet.

This book will accelerate the maximization of your full potential . . . quickly. In an age of doubters and fast food, the promise to maximize your potential quickly may seem like an inflated claim. However, just in the process of reading this introduction, you probably felt an actual sense of excitement resonating within yourself. Your instincts and intuition can tell the difference between truth and hype — you should be able to readily see that the ideas contained in *Let It Be Easy* will quickly produce marked results.

As much as possible, I try to integrate the information I am sharing with you now. But in all honesty, I have to also tell you that I have not attained absolute perfection. Since I am my own worst critic, I have to be watchful that I do not beat myself up when I see my own shortcomings. I, too, am constantly reminding myself to let it be easy.

Judged by outward appearances, most people would say I am a good example of everything I teach . . . and I am— most of the time. But who people *think* I am, is not who I am. However, it is who I *will be*, when I *become,* who it is people think I am.

4 simple points

+7 ingredients

---

11 powerful ideas

Let It Be Easy is built on eleven ideas. The first four, presented in the four chapters that follow, are simple points to remember. Then come the seven ingredients of an extraordinary life. Together they offer eleven actions you can initiate if you wish to obtain the most out of living. Simple, but powerful, these eleven ideas can make a profound difference in your daily experience. Read on to see how easy life can be if you let it.

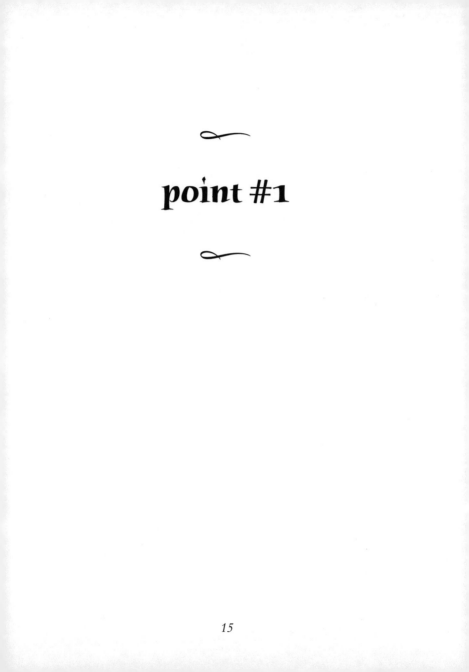

point #1

speak the truth

PEAKING THE TRUTH IS MORE THAN JUST A SOCIAL nicety. When you speak the truth as a commitment to your own personal growth, you actually align yourself with a tremendous power: *Truth*, with a capital "T." When you describe your feelings or relate something that you have experienced, you are speaking the truth. When you pass along gossip, you are not necessarily speaking the truth. Words have an amazing amount of power and you should constantly be watchful to see that your words are of service to yourself and others.

Speak truthfully about your own inner experience, and

your words will bring you closer to other people. This growing closer is a reflection of our instinctive love for sincerity. It's wonderful to be around someone when he or she says, "I just want to speak the truth about what I am feeling."

As you develop an ability to monitor what you say, you will discover that when you speak the truth you feel better about yourself and your relationships with others. People will recognize your integrity, and you will be regarded as someone who can be trusted. When you receive trust and respect, you tend to trust and respect others more easily and the entire quality of your day-to-day experience is enriched. Speaking the truth is ancient wisdom, and its power has been known for thousands of years. As you align yourself with Truth, your self-esteem will grow, and you will see respect constantly reflected back in the way people relate to you.

When you exaggerate, you are not speaking the truth. When you embellish your statements, you are not delivering accurate information. People often justify a "white lie" and fail to see that they are simply untruthful. It is possible to speak the truth and still be considerate of other people's feelings, instead of telling a white lie. For example, you can say, "she has a face that would stop a clock." Or you can say, "she has a face that makes time stand still."

Regain your personal power

I've heard people embellish and exaggerate to the point that they were actually delivering a bald-faced lie. Most of us usually label this kind of person a "bullshitter," and the person's credibility is sometimes irreversibly damaged. If you resemble this kind of person, please realize that you are reducing your personal power considerably. Ironically, this type of behavior is generally employed because a person is trying to make a better impression. The truth, of course, is that exaggerations can ordinarily be perceived for what they are, and rather than making a better impression, they diminish the speaker in the view of his listeners. You can assist yourself in developing impeccability in this area by addressing others who exaggerate with the simple inquiry, *"Is that accurate information?"*

Take Action Now!

This simple action will help ensure that you speak the truth.

- **Intend** to monitor and be aware of the things you say.

- **Notice** when you are not speaking the truth.

- **Re-mind** yourself when you have deviated from the path to personal power.

- **Correct** yourself out loud, if possible, by saying something like, "Well, actually that wasn't completely true — it really was like this."

People will immediately have more respect for you simply by witnessing your commitment to being truthful.

Let it be easy.

Speaking the truth feels far more comfortable than compromising your integrity. It also does wonders for your own self-esteem when you realize that others know you are a person who *always* speaks the truth.

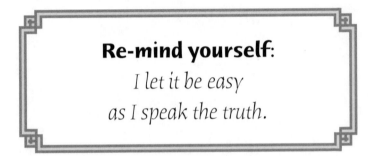

Re-mind yourself:
*I let it be easy
as I speak the truth.*

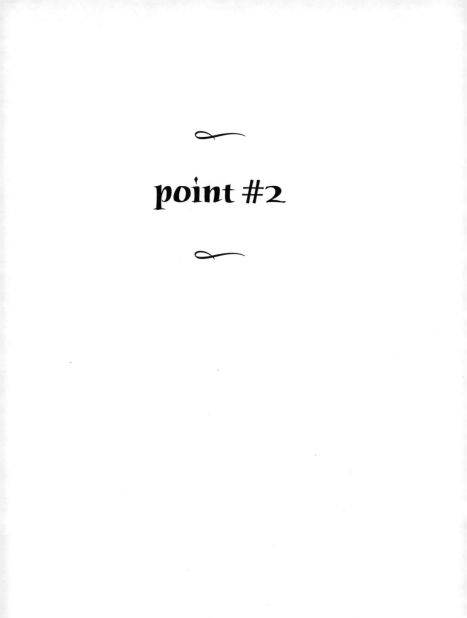

point #2

ask for what
you want

YOU CAN INSTANTLY REAP THE BENEFIT OF SPEAKING the truth by remembering this second important point: ask for what you want. At the table, you can ask someone — without experiencing guilt or feeling as though you are imposing — Will you pass the butter? That's easy, right? But why then do so many of us feel reluctant to ask for a shoulder massage when a nagging ache is causing our upper back to cramp? The truth is that you are more likely to receive what you want and need if you can speak up rather than play the role of a passive mute in pain. Truthfully asking for what you want demonstrates a healthy level of self-love that can transform your life.

Before you can ask for what you want, of course, you must know what you want. Unfortunately, most people go through life not really knowing what they want — they're just darn sure they don't have it. For instance, it is not good enough to simply say, "I want a better job." You must be specific. What does it pay? What are the hours? What's your supervisor like? The more specific you are, the more likely you are to get what you want.

I know a single mom who has two teenage boys. She never asked either of them for help around the house. She cooked the food, washed the dishes, did all the housekeeping, and collapsed in an exhausted heap at the end of each day. One afternoon while I was visiting, she was preparing to wash the windows. Both boys were upstairs playing video games. I said, "Jane, why don't you ask the boys to do the windows for you?" Her reply was, "Oh they're having fun upstairs, I don't mind." I'm not sure if she had a martyr-complex or what, but I called upstairs and said to the boys, "Your mom looks a bit tired, but the windows need to be cleaned. Why don't you guys help your mom and do the windows." They bounded down the stairs and with total joy set upon the task. They *kibitzed* and joked while they worked, and in no time at all, the windows were sparkling. The boys were actually delighted to make their mother's chores easier. I was simply amazed that Jane had never even thought to ask for help.

In fact, after witnessing the absolute enthusiasm the boys displayed at the opportunity to give something of value to their mom, I realized that she was actually serving her kids by allowing them to serve her.

The power in asking for what you want doesn't just relate to speaking with other people. You can also ask *silently.* Each morning, for example, before Jane even gets out of bed, she can ask for the experiences she wants to have in her day. She can visualize her kids feeling joyous as the family shares chores together. She can affirm

that her interactions with her boys will be light-hearted and filled with humor. She can pray that she and her sons grow closer.

Prayer, meditation, visualization and affirmations are all aspects of asking for what you want. The secret to attaining

your goal is persistence. Without being demanding and
without formulating conditions, keep focusing on what you
want. Ask for it. Don't torture yourself with impatience
and don't make your happiness dependant on whatever it
is you're asking for. You are simply making your needs and
wants known. This is the first step toward manifesting them.
Remember to ask for joy, peace and happiness, even before
you get out of bed. What kind of day are you going to give
yourself? And, *let it be easy.*

Think to ask

Of the four points to remember, this second point appears
too simple; it seems so obvious. Yet, in many subtle ways, we
overlook it completely. Some women never get the nurturing
they desire from their husbands. There's no reason for them
to have this dilemma. All they need is to ask for what they
want. "Stroke me here" or "touch me like this" may be all
the verbalization that it takes to bring about the results they
desire. Do not underestimate the power in being able to *ask
for what you want.*

  People often assume their request for something is going
to be turned down, so they never even make the request.

Take Action Now!

Practice asking for what you want by starting with a request for assistance.

Here is a suggestion for taking action:

- **Ask** someone to help you wash your car, paint your fence, or coach you on the delivery of a business presentation.

- **Re-mind** yourself how grateful you are to accept the help.

- **Notice** how you feel when you ask for what you want.

  - Do you feel stress?
  - Do you feel unworthy of what it is you are asking for?
  - Do you assume you will be refused even before you ask?
  - Do you feel great gratitude and appreciation?

If you are turned down:

- **Consider** if you could have made your request in another way.

- **Continue** by asking another person for assistance until you get what you asked for.

Keep practicing with simple requests until you feel completely comfortable asking for what you want.

Let it be easy.

Practice asking for what you want by starting with a request for assistance.

If you've never done this before, it may take a while until asking for what you want comes naturally, but this skill can bring greater comfort and ease into your life.

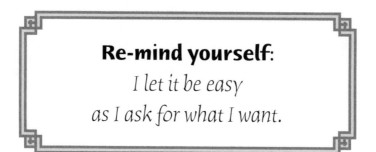

Re-mind yourself:

*I let it be easy
as I ask for what I want.*

point #3

keep your agreements

YOU ARE ADEPT AT SPEAKING THE TRUTH, AND YOU have mastered asking for what you want. Great! Now you can use these skills to assist you with the third point: keep your agreements. If you aren't truthful, can't say what you want or need, how can you ever come up with an agreement that you can keep? You set yourself up for failure.

With newfound understanding, you are now prepared to embrace the power of speaking the truth and asking for what you want, as you make your agreements with others and yourself. Promises and good intentions are wonderful, but if you aren't truthful about how much you can accomplish in a specific time frame, how can you keep an agreement? If you aren't able to ask for the support you need, you set yourself up for failure, and it is impossible to keep your agreements when large projects demand that you outsource certain tasks.

The nature of agreements

Once you make a commitment to yourself to keep your agreements, you will instantly notice whenever an agreement has been broken. For example, if you tell a friend that you will meet her at 4:30 and you do not arrive until 4:45, you will silently note that you have broken an agreement. You have created a small bump in what could have been a smooth road. By setting an intention to *keep your agreements,* you will see how much harmony or disharmony you are creating in your universe. This steadfastness may seem like a trivial point, yet when you are not respectful of even the most inconsequential agreement, the path of your life can never be completely easy.

As a parent, I have found it particularly rewarding to see how successful I've been in teaching this concept to my daughter Amber. Ever since she was born, she has witnessed the level of importance I have attached toward keeping my own agreements. When Amber would promise to clean her room, but failed to follow through, I would gently point out that she did not keep her agreement. I was never heavy-handed regarding this rule, but tried to help her understand the nature of agreements.

> I keep my agreements.

When we break an agreement, we contribute to the disappointment or disgust that others may have in reaction to our action or non-action. Many arguments, feuds and lawsuits are rooted in broken agreements. Agreements are sometimes called contracts and are written down. A handshake sometimes accompanies an agreement between two people. Agreements can be explicitly spoken, or simply implied.

The trust factor

Because agreements are based on trusting another person, when an agreement is broken, people often feel disrespected or betrayed. The feelings that are triggered in others when you break an agreement include anger, sorrow, panic, resentment, even rage. Why would you want to expose yourself to any of these emotions? When you see the link between broken agreements and negative emotions, you will be more motivated to create harmony in your life by being respectful of your agreements.

When you realize that you will not be able to keep an agreement, immediately contact the other party and renegotiate. Do this as soon as possible when it becomes obvious to you that you will not be able to do what you've said you would do. This contact is especially important with business appointments, college interviews and job interviews. The old cliché is still true: You will never get a second chance to make a first impression.

Take Action Now!

Here is a suggestion for a simple action to help you remember this third important point.

Focus on a simple agreement that you make all the time: promising to meet someone at a designated hour.

- **Make** a conscious effort to show up *exactly* on time. (Excuses for tardiness are not acceptable.)

- **Immediately** contact the person with whom you made the appointment if you sense that you are going to be late, and *renegotiate* your agreement.

- **Allow** for the unexpected. *Anticipate that there may be heavy traffic on the road, and leave early. Even if you plan your time and allow for traffic, there may still be unanticipated obstacles to prevent you from keeping your time agreement with someone. In that case, pull over and phone.*

> People will be appreciative of your sincere and genuine attempt to consider their feelings and their time. A simple phone call will make them realize that you respect them, and that you consider their time to be as valuable as your own. When you treat people with respect, you reap respect in return.
>
> ## Let it be easy.

When circumstances change

As you begin following through with your intention to keep all your agreements, those that are not kept will start feeling like an open safety pin in your underwear. Not a very comfortable image, is it? Well believe me, it feels *far worse* for the person with whom you have broken your agreement. Often this kind of discomfiture can be avoided. When you anticipate that an agreement cannot be kept — RENEGOTIATE. Circumstances frequently change, and most people realize this fact of life. When something occurs that makes it impossible for you to keep the original agreement, the honorable thing to do is to give as much advance warning as possible, and try to arrive at a new agreement that satisfies all parties concerned.

Personal power is not the result of any one action. It is the cumulative result of all your efforts and behavior. Never underestimate the power you can gain by keeping your agreements.

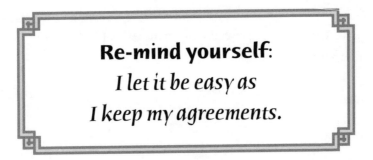

Re-mind yourself:
*I let it be easy as
I keep my agreements.*

point #4

take responsibility for your experiences

TOO OFTEN, WE THINK OTHER PEOPLE CAUSE US TO feel whatever it is that goes on inside us. "He made me angry" or "she makes my heart swell" are statements that deny how we create our own experiences. External events are merely stimulating situations. We are free to choose our own response to those situations. You are not a robot who must automatically respond a certain way when a specific button is pushed. You are free to select whatever response you desire.

The first three points I've suggested that you remember — speak the truth, ask for what you want, keep your agreements — will obviously enhance the quality of your life. However, the truly magical point is number four. As soon as you give up blaming others, you can start seeing reality with a new perspective. Instead of saying, "he made me angry," you can rephrase your experience by saying, "when he does that, I am reminded of similar situations from my past and I react with anger." In this way, you are taking responsibility for your experience *and* speaking the truth. Stop visualizing yourself as a victim. All that does is constantly make you feel helpless. As soon as you start accepting personal responsibility, you will realize that you can change any experience *internally*. Fred or Jim can do or say whatever they please, but you do not have to respond any certain way. *You* make yourself angry; *you* make yourself happy. You are the master of your own life. It's not what happens to you, it's what you *choose* to do about it.

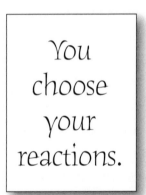

You choose your reactions.

Depending on where each person was raised, ten people in the same room can have ten different reactions to a given situation. *We each create our experience based on our past.* No one can presume to know what another person is experiencing. We can only be sure of our own experience. Because we are humans, we also have the ability to transform any experience we have. For example, if you are not enjoying yourself, you can choose to *learn* and *grow* from that situation. It is actually possible to use *every* circumstance for either pleasure or personal growth. In this way, you can never again lose in life. When you are choosing to enjoy yourself or grow in every moment, life becomes a constant adventure, never a battle.

Once you take responsibility for your own experience, you'll see how it is possible to change things in your life that you used to regret. The future will suddenly seem brilliant with infinite possibilities. You will be able to take control of your destiny and create whatever experiences you want.

In my seminars, I tell people that even though they may have played "victim" recently, they can now go back and learn from the situation by taking action in the present. I suggest to them that they do this:

Take Action Now!

1. On a sheet of paper, write down an incident from the recent past where you felt out of control.

2. Isolate the negative emotion that you felt in the situation, i.e. anger, humiliation, guilt, sorrow, despair. . .

3. Recall what thoughts were in your mind at the exact moment that you were experiencing those uncomfortable feelings. In other words, *what were you telling yourself?*

4. Imagine the entire drama as if you were actually watching it on a movie screen.

5. Now, rewrite the script and choose a new response. What might you have said to yourself that could have created a different experience?

6. In the future, practice doing this *as the movie is unfolding*, rather than at some later time.

If you follow this suggested action, you'll be able to rescue yourself from robot-like behavior, and enjoy the liberation and personal power that comes from creating your own experience. More and more, you'll begin realizing that your experiences are linked to what you are telling yourself. It is not what happens to you, it's your inner *response* that generates your feelings.

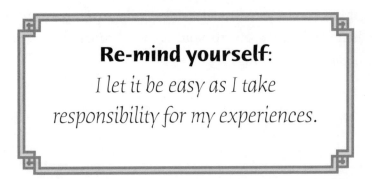

Re-mind yourself:

*I let it be easy as I take
responsibility for my experiences.*

7
ingredients of an extraordinary life

Being able to simply remember the four points that I just covered will improve your life even if you never finish reading the rest of this book. But if you truly desire to be as fulfilled as you can possibly be, check out the seven ingredients of an extraordinary life, which are outlined in the next seven chapters.

You can use *the four points to remember* as a way to add the seven ingredients of an extraordinary life to your own life — thus making your own life extraordinary.

Let it be easy.

add financial security to your life

I T IS IMPOSSIBLE TO GROW EMOTIONALLY AND BE HAPPY if your basic security needs aren't being met. Security means food, clothes and shelter. In today's society, these three things are equivalent to money. Money is a basic means of exchange that enables us to secure food, clothing and a home. If we do not have these three things, it is hard to be happy. It is difficult to encourage someone to seek anything else in life if he doesn't know where his next meal is coming from.

Of course, in our childhood these needs are provided by parents. However, most of us depend on a source of monetary income so that we can at least take care of ourselves. Before looking any further for happiness, examine your ability to provide yourself with basic sustenance.

Poor me

Fortunately, if you want help with your finances, we live in an age where seminars, books and classes abound. Using the Internet, or any other resource, you can get quality coaching to assist you in attaining financial well-being. If you are struggling with your budget, get some help. Until you feel financially secure, every other area of personal growth will seem difficult. However, you can certainly work on other areas while also creating financial health.

Regardless of how impoverished you may feel, there is always someone else whose situation is worse than your own. If you feel "poor," you encase yourself in a box created by your own thoughts. First and foremost, security, like everything else, is a reflection of your state of mind. It is imperative that you begin your journey toward financial security by first correcting your negative thoughts.

If you wish to feel wealthy right now, start practicing the time-tested ritual of tithing. No matter how little you have, you can afford to give away ten percent each week. Ten percent is a tiny sum and you will never notice any loss and will not feel any impact on your lifestyle.

When you tithe, you sub-consciously are telling yourself that you are wealthy enough to give money away. The amount is not important. What is important is that you stop thinking of yourself as "poor." All outward change begins with a change in thinking.

Rich me

Instead of spending all your time bemoaning your financial situation, now you will be spending some of your time pondering creative ways that you can give away money. You might *anonymously* give money to individual people, or you might support a charity that you favor. You can practice random acts of kindness by paying the toll for the person behind you at a bridge. Your own imagination is the only limitation on how you can give money away.

Take Action Now!

Address the issue of financial security in your life in four steps:

1. Speak the truth about your financial situation. Look at any stress caused by money shortages. Honestly express any dissatisfaction you feel about your finances.

2. Ask for what you want financially. This means you must accurately assess what it is you truly want, being as specific as possible. Go beyond what you need; explore what you want and allow yourself to indulge in the kinds of things money can provide.

3. Make a financial agreement with yourself and then keep your agreement. Agree to take actions that will create more financial security in your life. Set realistic target dates so you can evaluate your success. Then, keep your agreement by actually taking action.

4. Take responsibility for your financial experiences.

Let it be easy.

The process can be challenging, invigorating, stimulating, even fun . . . or *not*. You choose. You create the experience however you want by constructing the attitudes and affirmations beforehand.

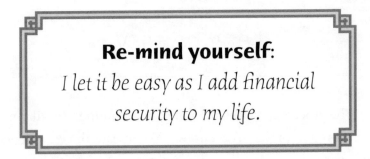

Re-mind yourself:
*I let it be easy as I add financial
security to my life.*

add good feelings
to your life

THE SECOND INGREDIENT OF AN EXTRAORDINARY LIFE is that it is filled with regularly occurring good feelings. Enjoyment might come from hiking, attending theater, having sex, eating, meditating, listening to music, traveling, laughing, sharing loving relationships, or almost any activity you find pleasant. Each morning you should be able to wake up and feel that life is good and worth living another day. Often we hear about people who have plenty of money and yet wind up killing themselves. Obviously, money alone cannot bring happiness. Day-to-day living should *feel* good. It is absolutely necessary if you want to be completely fulfilled.

If regular *good feelings* are missing from your life, you are going to experience it as "just not working." This dissatisfaction can be illustrated by a situation that happened in New York City. The late Hilda Charlton, a spiritual teacher in Manhattan, was approached after class by a young man who told her that he was extremely depressed.

"Why are you telling me this?" Hilda asked.

"I was hoping you could recommend something," he replied.

"If I tell you what to do, will you promise to do it?" Hilda responded.

"Sure," the young man said.

Hilda then told this fellow to stop at a grocery store on his way home, and to buy a chocolate cake mix, plus any other necessary ingredients needed to bake a chocolate cake. She instructed him to go home, bake the cake, allow it to cool, eat a large slice, and then phone her immediately.

Later that evening, Hilda's phone rang.

"Hello, Hilda, I just finished eating the cake."

"How do you feel?" Hilda asked.

"Great. I don't know what got into me, but I'm fine now."

An ancient truth is: *This too shall pass.* Sometimes it's just the absence of good feelings that brings about depression. Can you imagine anyone killing himself when he's feeling good? Don't underestimate the value of regular good feelings. They are a basic requirement of life. Don't deny yourself pleasure because you have some idea that it is decadent, unspiritual or selfish. Quite the contrary, bliss is a necessary part of growth. If you ever feel down, go to a funny movie or buy yourself a new shirt. Love yourself enough to do something nice for yourself.

Love yourself enough to do something nice for yourself.

When you are enjoying yourself, you are experiencing joy. Joyousness is a wonder-filled spiritual, experience. How many people do you know who seem like they experience a lot of joy? When you have joy in your life, it radiates out

Take Action Now!

If you suffer from a lack of regular good feelings, you can begin changing this situation immediately.

Use the **four points**:

1. Speak the truth and honestly acknowledge there are not enough good feelings in your life.

2. Ask for what you want. If you know what activities give you pleasure, make a list.

3. Keep your agreement by resolving to take a simple action that will make you feel good, each and every day.

4. Take responsibility for creating the experience you want to have as you add good feelings to your life. Some people receive great satisfaction from serving others. If you are one of these people, remember to also feel good about serving yourself.

Let it be easy.

and touches everyone you encounter. It not only nurtures the person experiencing the joy, but others as well. Feeling good is not indulgent, but a way of expressing appreciation for the abundance and beauty of life.

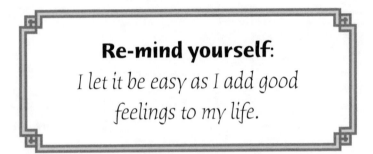

Re-mind yourself:
*I let it be easy as I add good
feelings to my life.*

add self-worth to your life

S OMETIMES, THE WAY WE CREATE GOOD FEELINGS IN our lives also provides us with financial security. A number of years ago, I had a friend, Barbara, who received a grant as part of the government's *Just Say No to Drugs* campaign. She was compensated for taking her puppet show into schools and performing a half-hour comedy with a message that discouraged kids from taking drugs. She told me many times how good she felt when she was doing her "work." Besides adding financial security and good feelings to her life, Barbara's actions also added self-worth to her life. It's extremely rewarding when our simple actions simultaneously add more than one ingredient that enriches our lives.

After satisfying our basic needs for security and good feelings, we must have a sense of self-esteem, free from guilt and unworthiness. Self-worth isn't to be confused with egotism or exaggerated pride; instead, it is a deep sense of our own value, uniqueness, and ability to perform effectively. People who don't have a positive self-image feel powerless to control their own destinies. They can have all the money and wonderful sensations imaginable, and yet they will never be happy. When we don't have self-worth, we are constantly threatened by people and situations around us, and are always defending ourselves and our territory. Whether we show it or not, we get angry easily, build ourselves up by putting others down, either verbally or mentally, and we still continue feeling bad about ourselves.

Value yourself

Self-worth means that you feel good about yourself, you respect yourself, you feel worthy of success, you have a sense that you are powerful enough to control your own destiny, and you feel okay about yourself even when other people put you down. Don't be confused by your impressions of people with "superiority complexes." There is no such thing as a superiority complex. People who always seek to build themselves up, or subtly put others down, do so because they are actually suffering from an "inferiority complex."

Self-worth means that you know you are *perfect* just the way you are and you accept yourself completely. Even if you are trying to improve yourself in certain areas, you start with the premise that it's perfect for you to begin from the point you're at now. You let go of guilt and stop regretting anything that is in the past. You recognize that you are a genuine expression of the universe, an aspect of the perfection that exists everywhere as the cosmos unfolds.

Can you possibly deny that the universe is perfect, *just the way it is?* You certainly cannot point to the night sky and say, "The universe is *almost* perfect, but that star is in the wrong place." You are a part of the perfect universe, just like any star, tree, stone or turtle.

An illustration

Imagine you are a housewife. While cooking the evening meal you become distracted by a phone call, and everything you prepared is burned to a crisp. Your husband comes home and attacks you with insults. "You are hopeless," he bellows. "You can't even boil water without burning it!"

If you don't have a sense of self-worth, you become intimidated by your husband's outburst and immediately retreat into feelings of guilt, shame and unworthiness. You forget who you really are. You forget that you are a perfect expression of a perfect universe. Suddenly, you begin to believe that you are a far cry from being perfect.

You are perfect even when you make "mistakes."

Well, if that were really the case, then obviously the community in which you live cannot be perfect; because when something is perfect, then every aspect and dimension of it must be perfect. A blemish or flaw in any portion of a thing mars its ultimate perfection. So now we must also deny the perfection of the continent on which you live. That continent is a part of the earth, so the planet

Earth can no longer be regarded as perfect. If we want to be completely accurate, we have to say that now the solar system of planets revolving around the sun is not perfect, because it includes *you*. The sun is only one of billions of stars in our galaxy known as the Milky Way, and now we have to label the entire galaxy as imperfect. This galaxy represents only a tiny fraction of all the galaxies that comprise the universe. So it is easy to see that the universe can't possibly be perfect; because woven into the cosmic fabric, there *you* are.

When seen from this vantage point, it becomes ludicrous to see yourself as ever being less than perfect. The universe really is perfect just the way it is, and it includes *you*. In fact, right now, it wouldn't be the same *without* you. No matter who you are or what you do, you can acknowledge your self-worth because you are always part of a perfect universe. Never forget that regardless of your actions or other people's judgments of you, your perfection remains unchanged.

Forgiveness: the magic ingredient

It is important to forgive yourself for anything you have done in the past. Everyone makes mistakes, and our greatest lessons are generally byproducts of our greatest mistakes.

This is how we grow — from trial and error. Thomas Edison never saw his failures as mistakes. He has been quoted as saying, that over the years, he simply learned 1,000 ways not to make a light bulb. The past is gone and exists only in your mind. Each day you are born anew, and guilt or unworthiness based on the past can never make a positive contribution to your life or anyone else's.

Trial + Error = Growth

Mistakes are a part of the process involved in finding yourself. If you regret something you said or did, notice that you may have behaved inappropriately, learn the lesson you need to learn, and resolve to act more appropriately next time. You are perfect even when you make "mistakes."

So far, I've addressed the first three of seven ingredients in an extraordinary life. We must have our security needs met, we have to supply ourselves with regular good feelings, and we need a sense of self-worth.

Sometimes humans behave as if they absolutely need the approval of others in order to survive. If someone criticizes us, or disapproves of our actions, we frequently react as if our very survival is being threatened. Four-legged animals do not seem to waste time doing this. Can you imagine a squirrel anguishing that there are not enough good feelings around and contemplating suicide? Do you suppose squirrels experience lingering feelings of unworthiness? If a squirrel ransacks your flower bed and you charge at it shouting *"No! No! Scram! Bad! Bad! Go away!"* I guarantee you that this squirrel will not lose one night of sleep. Squirrels feel perfectly all right with their "squirrelness."

Animals spend little energy focusing on these first three ingredients of a fulfilling life, and yet these needs are satisfied. Animals are content with what they are, and live lives in cadence with a certain rhythm. Actually, the first three ingredients are easy to attain. Yet most humans go through life struggling with them, hoping to someday experience the same fulfillment that squirrels enjoy.

Take Action Now!

You can assist yourself in developing self-worth by making a list of all the traits, qualities and characteristics you possess that you feel good about.

This is not an exercise in humility. Pat yourself on the back.

- Write down as many positive traits as you can.

Now:

- **List** of all the things you regret: your words, deeds and actions from the past.

- **Start** at the beginning of your completed list and say out loud: *Healed and forgiven!*

- **Respond** orally to each item on the list, cross the item out with a large marking pen and resolve never to think about it again.

- **Read** again your list of positive traits; it should make you feel good about yourself.

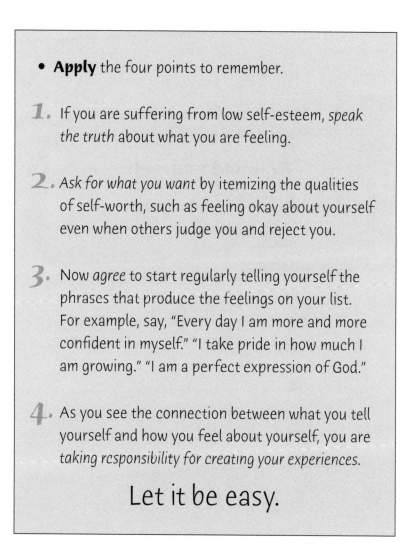

- **Apply** the four points to remember.

1. If you are suffering from low self-esteem, *speak the truth* about what you are feeling.

2. *Ask for what you want* by itemizing the qualities of self-worth, such as feeling okay about yourself even when others judge you and reject you.

3. Now *agree* to start regularly telling yourself the phrases that produce the feelings on your list. For example, say, "Every day I am more and more confident in myself." "I take pride in how much I am growing." "I am a perfect expression of God."

4. As you see the connection between what you tell yourself and how you feel about yourself, you are *taking responsibility for creating your experiences.*

Let it be easy.

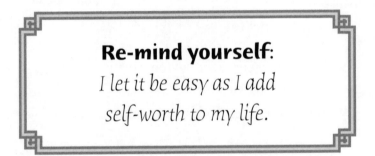

Re-mind yourself:
*I let it be easy as I add
self-worth to my life.*

life requirements:

1. Financial security
2. Good feelings
3. Self-worth

These first three ingredients are basic. They are *life requirements*. We have them in common with all the other mammals walking the earth. Now, let's examine the next four ingredients — the ones that are only available to humans — and can truly make your life an extraordinary experience.

add active compassion to your life

A CTIVE COMPASSION IS A CALL TO ACTION. THIS quality stems from love — not the stereotyped love portrayed in romantic novels, but the love that flows out of us and results in good deeds directed toward other people.

The love that makes our hearts go pitter-pat and causes our loins to twitch isn't love, but a sensation, and belongs in the category of good feelings. The love that is the source of *active compassion* allows us to forgive the past, both for ourselves and others. It enables us to forget the pettiness and traumas of yesterday. Our love for our mates, our children, and our friends is only the beginning. The love that forms the basis of active compassion is an embodiment of succeeding with the first three ingredients of an extraordinary life and loving ourselves enough to let energy flow through our hearts. As this state unfolds within us and becomes full, humility and compassion are natural results.

Receiving by giving

Active compassion is synonymous with charity. It is a way of receiving through giving. It is serving others because we have feelings of goodwill toward our fellow human beings and know that they are serving us by allowing us to serve them. Until we start performing good deeds for their own sake, not for praise or for other personal rewards, or because we *think* we should, we can't progress up the path toward total happiness. It is possible to garner moments of pleasure from life if we add the first three ingredients alone, but Joy with a capital "J" comes only after we consider someone else's needs to be as important as our own. Of course, it is essential to first love oneself, so that you are not serving others in order to compensate for what you consider to be your own inadequacies. Active compassion is love flowing forth as service.

Distinctly human

I only understood what active compassion meant after I became a parent. It was the first time I felt that another person's needs were not just as important as my own, but, oftentimes, even more important. This type of love is a distinct human quality. Human beings have within themselves the capacity to be unconditionally loving. The key is to discover what it means to be *unconditional* in the way you express your love.

When you are able to accept someone unconditionally, you are practicing the ancient teaching that Jesus taught his followers. He told them that they must love their enemies; because if they only loved the people who were nice to them, then his followers were really only doing what everyone else was doing. His call to love *unconditionally* was a radical departure from what was commonly thought to be natural human behavior. We all possess the ability to be unconditionally loving and forgiving. This quality of love means that you can serve and accept everyone — including yourself.

The love now being described doesn't even have to be directed at people. Selfless service can be expressed by simply picking litter off the street. This kind of love is incredible medicine; you can practice it anywhere, at any time, and it will always create "goodness" and have the effect of making you feel good about yourself. Service to others is an excellent remedy for depression; whenever you're feeling down, do something nice for another and you will start feeling better about yourself.

Giving
feels
good.

There is no limitation on how you can serve. You can tithe, you can volunteer, you can visit an elderly shut-in, you can read to a blind person, you can water plants for a vacationing neighbor, you can walk a buddy's dog while he's sick, you can remove graffiti from public places, or you can do whatever else might occur to you. Giving in this way is really receiving. It appears as if you are serving someone else; but the truth is, they are serving you by allowing you to serve them.

This quality of love is a lot different from just having loving feelings that remain unexpressed.

The distinction is made clear in the story of a young man who was addicted to constantly immersing himself in pleasurable sensations. On his walls he had numerous pictures of nude women, and every evening he would return from work, smoke pot and watch porno movies. His bookshelves were cluttered with bottles of alcohol and pornographic magazines. He loved to seduce women into one-night sex marathons. Whenever he could afford it, he bought cocaine.

Finally, a friend of his, who had recently converted to Christianity, chided him about his amoral and hedonistic lifestyle. On an impulse, the fellow responded by resolving to change himself. He began going to church, and he took a trip to Jerusalem.

When he returned from his vacation in the Holy Land, it was obvious to all who knew him — here was a changed man. He had completely eliminated alcohol, drugs and pornography from his life. He didn't just redecorate his apartment, he adorned it with pictures of Jesus and inspirational scenes from the Bible. Every evening, after work, he lit a candle and meditated. This activity went on for many months. "I have really transformed," the young man often thought to himself. "I have become so spiritual and loving."

However, in all those months, this man did not do one thing that was motivated by selfless thoughts. Though he may have inspired others with his outer transformation, his intention was never to serve anyone else but himself. He merely found another way of creating good feelings. He substituted one set of pleasurable sensations for another collection of sensations. Doubtless, his meditations, prayers and loving feelings are better for him than what he was doing before — and he is definitely pointed in the right direction — but until he goes out into the world and does something for the benefit of another, until he uses his newfound energy to improve the quality of someone else's life, until he expresses what he is experiencing internally by out-flowing it in the form of service, it is not the love I call active compassion. It is still good feelings.

Obviously, the boy's family was delighted with his changes for the better. The boy's original ways of giving himself good feelings were unhealthy compared to the ways he gave himself good feelings now. If the boy focused on how his behavior was nurturing his family, then he would be closer to active compassion.

But as long as he focuses on himself and is oblivious to how he is affecting his family — even though his effect is good — he is not acting from compassion. Often, outer actions may appear similar, even when performed by people in completely different mental states and motivated by conflicting intentions.

> If you don't have love, it doesn't matter what else you have.

Some people manage to effortlessly add the first three ingredients of an extraordinary life. They have ample wealth, considerable amounts of pleasurable stimulation, and a strong degree of self-worth. However, if they do not have a deep, experiential sense of what love really means, everything else seems hollow. In one way or another, poets have always told us, "If you don't have love, it doesn't matter what else you have." (And remember, without the underlying foundation of the first three ingredients, love may occasionally shimmer across your horizon, but then it's gone. To be in a position to effectively serve, it is best to first securely anchor yourself — so you have the strength and resources to support the needs of others.)

Take action now!

Add active compassion to your life. Using your creative imagination, devise a way in which you can be of service.

- **Write** down several possibilities. Your selfless service can be a one-time project, or it can be a commitment to something ongoing. You can serve a person, or a good cause.

- **Choose** one that seems the most attractive to you right now.

- **Apply** the four points:

1. *Speak the truth;* be honest with yourself about the type of service that you're willing and able to take on now.

2. *Ask for what you want:* Contact the person or agency involved and tell them what you want to do. Ask someone to help you if necessary.

3. *Keep your agreement.* Show up and perform the service.

4. Take responsibility for this experience. Feel satisfaction about adding active compassion to your life. Tell yourself, "I've done a good thing."

Let it be easy.

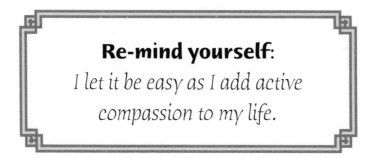

Re-mind yourself:
I let it be easy as I add active compassion to my life.

add creative expression to your life

THE FIFTH INGREDIENT IS VERY SUBTLE. EVEN WHEN the first four are part of your life, and you are basically happy, days can sometimes seem flat and without sparkle. *Creative expression* is like perfume or seasoning added to something that is already rather satisfying. When it is absent, we can feel frustrated for no apparent reason.

Whether this creativity comes in the form of music, sewing, gardening, dance, art, song, writing, sports, or some other hobby or vocation, including business, we must somehow unlock our creative capacity. Otherwise, we can lapse into boredom. Our need for creative expression is rarely considered, and when it is missing, many people can't even guess where the problem lies. Yet, when creativity manifests itself in full bloom, it enhances one's life as if by magic.

If you are seeking nothing less than complete fulfillment as a human being, you must have a way of expressing your creativity. It is also possible for life's ingredients to overlap or coincide. The way in which we channel our creativity can also be the way in which we serve others or earn a living.

> Creative expression is a necessary part of living. Make time for it.

Creative expression can also be a source of good feelings. When this occurs, life is experienced as a cornucopia from which we always have more than we need. The inner sensation of this experience is one of abundance and fulfillment; your *life itself* then becomes your creative expression.

Barbara, the puppeteer, is again a perfect example of this fulfillment, as she performs her consciousness-raising skits at public schools. The theme of her puppet show improves the quality of kids' minds. At once, all five ingredients we've mentioned are simultaneously covered. How wonderful for Barbara, since her creative expression is also compassionate service.

I once encouraged a woman, Charlotte, to express her love of gardening more creatively. For years she had grown organic vegetables for herself and her neighbors, but her garden was a clutter of wheelbarrows, tools, compost heaps and discarded tangles of wire fencing. It was bereft of beauty. When I pointed out that adding flowers would create more beauty in her garden, Charlotte responded with astonishment that the idea hadn't occurred to her years before.

Twelve months later, Charlotte's garden was transformed. Gone was all the clutter. Magnificent flowerbeds and flowering vines were everywhere. Charlotte's garden was breath-taking. She became so creative, and had so much fun in her garden, soon friends joined her for the sheer joy of participating in the creation of so much beauty. One result was that the garden began producing more and more organic vegetables. Charlotte sold her excess veggies, making a nice profit. Again we see how creativity and all the other ingredients we are discussing can intertwine.

Take action now!

Starting immediately, inject creativity into your life.

- **Write** down a list of creative activities you enjoy, or would like to try.

- **Set aside** the time. If you enjoy acting, join a local theater group. If you like to sing, join a chorus. If you want to play an instrument, enroll in a class. If you have natural talent as an artist, earmark several hours a week to paint or draw. Whatever form of creative expression tickles your fancy, take action by making time to include this in your life.

- **Apply** the four points:

1. *Speak the truth* about the creative expression, or lack of it, in your life.

2. *Ask for what you want.*

3. *Keep your agreement* with yourself. Regardless of how busy you are and no matter how cramped your schedule, realize that creative expression is a necessary part of living, and make time for it.

4. *Take responsibility* for your creative experiences by lavishing some praise on yourself.

Let it be easy.

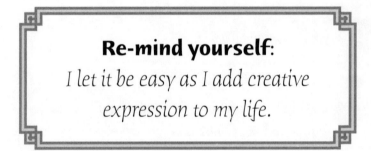

Re-mind yourself:
I let it be easy as I add creative expression to my life.

the spiritual dimension

If you are feeling anxious, grievous, blocked, depressed or bored, carefully examine your life and see what's missing. Are you serving others in some way? Are you expressing your creativity? There can be no doubt that if you add the first five ingredients, you will be a very happy person. Being happy is not difficult; it's actually quite easy once you learn how to do it. Yet, being happy is not the ultimate goal in being alive. Beyond happiness, there is a spiritual dimension to life. The sixth and seventh ingredients of an extraordinary life are specifically concerned with spirituality.

add attentive awareness
to your life

J UST BEFORE THIS POINT IS REACHED, WE MAY FEEL HAPPY enough that we lack any great incentive to explore the remaining two areas of personal growth. We're missing the best part of life if we don't explore them, however.

The sixth area — *attentive awareness* — can help us develop a profound dimension to happiness. This aspect connects us directly to our inner spiritual nature. If we only satisfy our yearnings for the first five ingredients, although we may feel nourished, we may still remain uneasy when the subjects of birth, death, God, or inexplicable phenomena are discussed in our presence.

Learning how to practice attentive awareness moment by moment is perhaps the most basic part of spiritual development. The attentive awareness I am describing is not a casual state of mind. When I refer to attentiveness as a tool for spiritual growth, I mean paying attention *one hundred percent*. When you pay attention *completely*, life is transformed. When you pay attention to the smell of a flower one hundred percent, you *become* the smell of the flower. When you pay attention — one hundred percent — to the taste of food, you *become* the taste of the food.

How often do you sit at the dinner table watching television and never tasting the meal you are eating? How frequently do you consume your dinner thinking about the events of the day or worrying about appointments and bills? Only when you are not distracted can you fully experience the richness of the food in your mouth.

The power of paying attention: an example

A monk is hiking through the jungle when suddenly a tiger leaps in his path. The monk turns and flees until he finally comes to a steep cliff. Growing along the edge of the cliff is a long vine. He immediately descends the vine, but when he looks down, he discovers two tigers waiting for him at the base of the vine. Of course, by now, there are several tigers looking down at him from above. If the situation isn't bad enough, two mice start chewing through the vine just out of his reach. Suddenly, the monk notices a wild strawberry growing from the side of the cliff. He plucks the strawberry and pops it into his mouth.

The traditional story ends here. Rather than stop now, however, let's look at the story's implications.

When the monk popped the strawberry into his mouth, he instantly paid attention to the taste of the strawberry. He paid attention *100 percent!* When you pay attention — *100 percent* — to the taste of food, you *become* the taste. Therefore, the monk *became* the strawberry, and of course, he never had an experience of being eaten by the tigers.

The story of the tigers and the strawberry is symbolic. Life is always sending us tigers and always sending us strawberries. For example, if you are a non-smoker and are sitting near the smoking section of a restaurant, you can become very upset because the smoke is drifting across your table. The smoky air can be the tiger. If you do not wish to suffer, however, you can look for a strawberry on which to focus your attention. Perhaps there is a glorious sunset you can watch through the window. If you focus your attention — one hundred percent — on the sunset, you can instantly up-level your experience from one of suffering to one of joy.

Life is always handing you "tigers" and always handing you "strawberries." It's up to you to choose what you want to experience. When you feel miserable, it's only because you are paying attention to the tigers. At that moment, you have to find a strawberry and pay attention to *it* one hundred percent.

Fully conscious

When you cultivate this ability to focus your attention one hundred percent, you will become your own best teacher. You will be able to learn from situations you never even noticed before. So many problems are just byproducts of not paying attention. Children spill milk as the result of not paying attention. Someone may fall down a flight of stairs because they are not paying attention. Litter, war, pollution and prejudice are all a result of not paying attention. In fact, when you are behind the wheel of a car, paying attention can literally save your life.

Paying attention to your thoughts will reveal how *you yourself* create most of your problems. Paying attention to your habits, actions and relationships will give you insights that will add to your personal power and effectiveness in the world. For example, make a conscious decision to pay attention to a certain habit you'd like to control. Perhaps you inject the words "ya' know" or "ya' see" or "um" as you talk, and you really want to clean those extraneous utterances from your way of speaking. It's a small thing, but let's start with something easy.

As you begin to pay attention, you'll notice more and more every time those unconscious interjections occur in your speech. Don't judge yourself or even try to change the habit. Just continue to pay attention.

Before long, the habit will have corrected itself as if by magic. You will not have to make any conscious effort to do anything at all to bring about the results you desire. All you do is begin to pay attention in a new way, and your life suddenly improves.

You can select any habit at all. It can be a nervous twitch, a habit of interrupting people when they are speaking, or a habit of eating when you're not really hungry. However, just

Focus on one thing.

use one thing to work on at any given time, and choose something relatively minor. Start with something easy as you begin to familiarize yourself with this step toward personal power and spiritual attainment.

Using attentive awareness, each person can look within and discover his or her own inner truth. As we pay attention to who we are within — spirituality evolves. Attentive awareness kindles a spiritual awakening that results in "ordinary" moments no longer seeming so ordinary.

Attentive awareness enables us to cope with life's seemingly contradictory and paradoxical nature. It enables us to be aware of our egos and see them clearly. It permits us to step back from the melodrama of our lives and watch it all unfold as if on a movie screen. It creates the needed detachment to laugh at our own foibles and shortcomings.

Quite simply, attentive awareness, the sixth ingredient for an extraordinary life, guides us into being aware that we are aware. This creates a bridge into the purely spiritual dimension, and allows us to see our true nature as being separate from the cycle of birth, life-scramble and death. The fulfillment that accompanies attentive awareness is so far above the satisfaction provided by the first five ingredients, that it resembles it no more than a butterfly resembles a caterpillar.

Paying attention represents an entirely new way of "seeing." Attentive awareness enables us to literally unite with whatever we are experiencing in any given moment. When you eat — pay attention! When you wash dishes — pay attention! When you use the bathroom — pay attention!

Be a witness

Attentive awareness eventually gives birth to the spiritual quality of non-attachment. Soon, it no longer matters what it is that you are paying attention to; suddenly you are able to perceive that you are a spiritual witness to everything occurring around you — as if you are in the audience, watching a movie. You begin to sense that you are in the world, but not of it. You can detach yourself so that you are no longer like a robot, instantly reacting to whatever pushes your buttons.

In this mode, everything and anything has the potential for becoming a spiritual experience. Even pain can become a spiritual experience, once you separate yourself from the pain by "witnessing" it. Although animals can be aware of pain, only human beings have the ability to be detached — to be aware that they are aware. As you practice being aware that you are aware, through attentive awareness, it no longer matters what

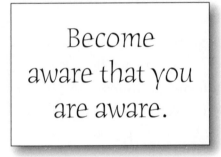

Become aware that you are aware.

"movie" is actually playing. You are detached to the point that it no longer matters whether it's a comedy or a tragedy on the screen of your awareness. You sense that who you really are is the watcher. Even your own body is seen as something on the screen. You begin experiencing what has always been referred to as your soul — the immortal part of yourself that lies beyond birth and death.

When you practice this detachment, events are no longer "good" or "bad." Everything just "is." You watch the movie without judgment and are able to make conscious decisions without reacting from habit to whatever is happening on the screen of your life.

Consider the spirituality of the poor man whose horse runs away. His neighbor sighs, "How unfortunate you are." But the man only replies with, "Maybe." The next day, the horse returns, leading an entire herd into the man's corral. As the man closes the gate, the neighbor exclaims, "How lucky you are." Again, the man's only reply is, "Maybe." Several days later, the man's son attempts to ride one of the wild horses and breaks his leg. The neighbor laments, "What a tragedy." Of course, the man only says, "Maybe." Shortly thereafter, a war is declared and the man's son is exempted from military service because of his badly fractured leg. "How fortunate," declares the neighbor.

"Maybe."

The spiritual awareness and non-attachment that this man displays is born of "watching." Attentive awareness transmutes life into a constantly active process of meditation. Once you become self-aware, you will sense a spiritual presence that is always with you and within you. . . always watching. . . aware of everything that you are aware of. The watcher sees what you see, hears what you hear, smells what you smell, feels what you feel, experiences what you experience. An entirely new dimension of life unfolds as a result of cultivating attentive awareness.

As you do this more and more, you will become aware that you are aware.

When you are bored, you can observe that you are lacking creative expression. When you are enjoying sex, you can notice that good feelings are present. When you are doing nothing in particular, pay attention to whatever is around you in the moment. Notice how often you automatically react to situations as if you are a robot, with no ability to make a conscious choice about how you would like to respond. For example, someone cuts you off in traffic, and you instantly shout something obscene.

Take Action Now!

Take action by beginning the practice of paying attention to yourself and your feelings.

- **Witness** the feeling the other person's behavior creates in you.

- **Notice** that you are separate from your feelings.

- **Observe** the uncomfortable feelings, then observe yourself observing yourself.

- **Detach** yourself from your own thoughts and feelings.

- **Realize** that you are capable of being an observer of your own life-movie.

- **Create** a new spiritual dimension from which you can observe your life.

Let it be easy.

In time you will see that most people around you are clueless when it comes to creating this spiritual dimension from which to observe life. You will soon be chuckling about how robotic people are. You will note that most others — trapped in the movie with no ability to detach themselves — have no choice in how they behave, while you see yourself as *in* the movie, but not *of* it.

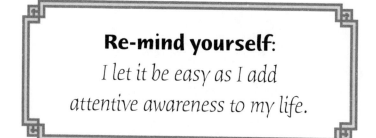

Re-mind yourself:

*I let it be easy as I add
attentive awareness to my life.*

connect to a higher power

AFTER YOU HAVE SPENT TIME PRACTICING ATTENTIVE awareness, something amazing will happen; you will start experiencing more and more frequently that you are *constantly* connected to the Source that created you. In fact, you *are* always connected to the Earth, the solar system, the stars, the universe. You are connected, whether you realize it or not, to everything that exists. As a human being, you have the potential to *experience* your connection to *All That Is*, which many refer to simply as God. *You* are a part of *that!*

We frequently hear, "we are one," sung in songs and written in books. What does that mean? It means there is only one unified energy everywhere. *You* are a part of *that!* All the power of the universe is at your disposal. How soon will you grasp that you have never at any time been separate from the source of your creation?

God
is all
that is.

The seventh ingredient for an extraordinary life is the most elusive, and, therefore, the most difficult to describe. So few people incorporate it into their lives that it is rare to find an effective role model. When attained, this mode of living — constantly feeling connected to every person and thing on the planet, experiencing a connection to the Power of the entire universe — enables a person to perceive not merely the world of solid objects, but the bundles of energy and particles appearing as form. Nothing lies beyond our comprehension if we discover and develop this aspect of our nature. As students of life, it stands before us as a monument to our potential as human beings, and explains to us all the powers attributed to the saints and sages throughout history.

God is all that is. Since everything that exists is God, in one form or another, the only way that God can make a tree is by *becoming* the tree. Likewise, the way God made you was by *becoming* you.

You will discover that a constant connection to this Higher Power acts like a soothing balm, healing every aspect of your life. It is the Joy — with a capital "J" — that sprouts from speaking the truth, asking for what you want, keeping your agreements, taking responsibility for your experiences, and creating a life that has security, good feelings, self-worth, active compassion, creative expression and attentive awareness.

Take Action Now!

Take action now through the practice of remembering how God created you.

- **Allow** God to appreciate the sunset through your eyes.

- **Acknowledge** that it is God listening to the birds through your ears.

- **Know** that you will continue to grow as you develop a deep inner sense of your constant connectedness to the source of creation, and all that is.

- **Discover** how a constant connection to this Higher Power acts like a soothing balm, healing every aspect of your life.

By embracing your connection to the Higher Power you access the Joy — with a capital "J" — that sprouts from speaking the truth, asking for what you want, keeping your agreements, taking responsibility for your experiences, and creating a life that has security, good feelings, self-worth, active compassion, creative expression and attentive awareness.

Let it be easy.

No doubt, Frances of Assisi was experiencing this connection when he said:

Make me an instrument of your peace.
Where there is hatred, let me sow love;
Where there is injury, pardon;
Where there is doubt, faith;
Where there is despair, hope;
Where there is darkness, light;
Where there is sadness, joy.
Grant that I may not so much seek to be consoled, as to console;
To be understood, as to understand;
To be loved, as to love
For it is in giving that we receive;
It is in pardoning that we are pardoned;
And it is in dying that we are born to eternal life.

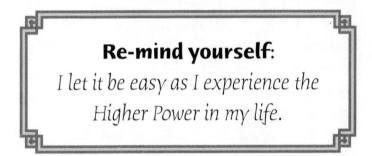

Re-mind yourself:

I let it be easy as I experience the Higher Power in my life.

live in a new reality

I F YOU ARE EARNEST IN YOUR COMMITMENT TO YOUR own psychological and emotional growth, the way you approach living should be completely supportive of your personal evolution. Right diet, right action and right company are vital areas demanding your attention. It is imperative that you create a quality lifestyle that is conducive to growth and transformation.

Imagine living in a huge city with millions of people. At five o'clock rush hour, the underground subway system becomes unbearably congested. You arrive at a subway entrance ten minutes before five o'clock and descend several long flights of stairs. As you puff your way around a corner at the base of the last flight, a sign appears: "This entrance closed. Use entrance across the street." You think, *certainly there must have been a similar sign at the top of these stairs. The wind probably blew it away.*

With a few deep breaths, you resolutely prepare for your ascent. Halfway up the stairs, however, you encounter the five o'clock rush hour throng pouring down the tiled stairwell. Thousands of people are descending; and you try to tell them that at the bottom of the stairs, the subway entrance is barricaded. It's hopeless, of course. They swarm past you like an army of ants.

At this point, you find it quite difficult to proceed with your ascent. In fact, not only is it hard to move forward, you might even feel that it is more sensible to turn around and move in the direction of the masses, even though you know it's a dead end.

The imagery here points to the advantage of being in the company of people who are heading in the same direction that you want to go. Surrounding yourself with the right company is extremely important, especially when you are just beginning the journey of personal development.

When you associate with people who are critical of your practices and are not supportive of your desire for personal evolution, you're placing yourself at a severe disadvantage. A healthy environment that includes the right company is as important as healthy food.

Support your growth

When you plant a small tree, it is wise to erect a fence around it so that animals don't eat it and people don't inadvertently trample it. When the tree grows large enough, the fence can then be removed since the tree can easily stand on its own. Care for yourself in a similar way.

Support yourself by seeking the company of people who are also dedicated to personal growth. Surround yourself with a community of conscious friends. By having a network of emotional support in your life, you'll get touched, and hugged, and listened to, whenever you need it.

Release negative influences from your life. Disengage from people who are constantly negative or perpetually critical and destructive with their words, thoughts and deeds. Only after you regard yourself as a pillar of strength, may you wish to return to that type of company to perhaps show them a better way of living.

Simplify your life!

It is also important to remember that your actions always create reactions. This is a simple law of cause and effect. Once you take personal responsibility for creating your life, you must be constantly watchful that you don't create what you don't want through actions that will have negative repercussions. As you become more aware of your own thoughts, and watch yourself talking and moving in the world, you will see a connection between what you sow and what you reap. Kind people seem to live in a friendly world, and angry people seem to live in a hostile world.

Simplify your life. Why burden yourself with the stress that accompanies huge mortgage payments you can't really afford emotionally, revolving charge plans, and expenses resulting from costly playthings? As we grow in consciousness, material possessions become less and less important. Simplification of lifestyle, just like simplification of diet, produces optimal health. Examine your life and see how you can simplify it.

You can use love, joy, nurturing friends, laughter and happiness as measures of your success. Don't use money as a measure of your success.

Many people allow the quality of their lives to deteriorate because their financial prosperity has misled them into believing that they were winning, when they were actually losing. Should a person consider himself

New measures of success

a success if he has earned several million dollars, but his diet, personality and lifestyle have resulted in his having ulcers, hypertension, cardiac deficiencies and miserable relationships?

Because Westerners have been intensely conditioned to equate monetary gain with success, we have compromised our entire culture by polluting the environment and destroying the minds and morale of countless millions. So long as the economy prospers, our governments tell us there is cause for celebration. Nonsense! Through simplification of lifestyle and a reordering of your priorities, you can create heaven on Earth everyday. Once you realize how little money is really needed to survive, you can spend more time dancing, running through the forest, hugging your children, and enjoying hobbies, sports and pastimes. Don't confuse quantity with quality.

Train yourself to be consistently optimistic and positive in your thinking. Even when diet and exercise are deficient, right thinking can maintain perfect health. A positive mental attitude can keep you looking young and radiant when others your age are old and wrinkled. There are no limits to this power.

Above all else, rely on positive thinking as your vehicle for attaining your goals — nothing is strong enough to resist you when you keep your mind focused on love, happiness and joy. Instead of lamenting that roses have thorns, why not rejoice that thorns have magnificent flowers adorning them? Replace your doubt with positivity and you will notice immediate changes in your experience of living. Research has clearly shown that our entire body chemistry can be changed by changing our thoughts.

Easy living

By embracing the four points and the seven ingredients, in time, you will discover that you are living in an entirely new reality. You will notice more and more people approaching you wanting to know what your secret is. By practicing the principles outlined in this book, you will add years to your life and more zest to your years.

The simple actions in *Let It Be Easy* provide you with a way of monitoring your life. Do this in a casual manner so you don't become over-critical of yourself. *Let it be easy!* View your progress on the path of personal development as being similar to a rocket. When rockets are launched to the moon or to Mars, they are always off course. Computers are continually monitoring the rocket's progress, and constantly correcting to the right, then to the left. As a result of the self-correcting guidance system, the rocket eventually arrives on target. Using the tools provided in this book, you too now have a way of examining yourself so that you will know when you are off course. Practice gently correcting yourself so that you can arrive at your target — *your full potential.*

When you discover that you are reverting to old

behavior that causes discomfort, don't condemn yourself for failing. If you catch yourself and correct the behavior, you haven't failed — you've learned something. This is the way we grow. Every situation, enjoyable or otherwise, can assist us in becoming more effective.

Set your life up so that you can never lose; if you aren't completely comfortable with yourself, learn the lesson or insight that will prevent you from repeating the ineffective behavior. In this way, you are either always content, or you are learning lessons that will help you grow.

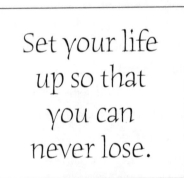

Set your life up so that you can never lose.

Reading a menu is only a hint of the pleasure that awaits you when you actually eat the meal that has been described. This book is very similar to a menu. Regardless of how much you enjoyed reading about the extraordinary life awaiting you, the result of implementing these ideas is vastly more enjoyable than you can possibly imagine.

Every adventure begins with one step. As you close the book, take a step toward becoming the extraordinary person you were meant to be.

ELEVEN ACTIONS TO CREATE AN EXTRAORDINARY LIFE

- *Speak the Truth*

- *Ask for What You Want*

- *Keep Your Agreements*

- *Take Responsibility for Your Experiences*

- *Add Financial Security to Your Life*

- *Add Good Feelings to Your Life*

- *Add Self-Worth to Your Life*

- *Add Active Compassion to Your Life*

- *Add Creative Expression to Your Life*

- *Add Attentive Awareness to Your Life*

- *Connect to a Higher Power*

THE TWELFTH ACTION TO CREATE AN EXTRAORDINARY LIFE

- *Give copies of this book to your circle of friends. Let it be easy together!*

About the Author

During the 1970s, Tolly Burkan created innovate, cutting-edge methods for developing human potential. As a result of his pioneering strategies, seminars focusing on his work are now offered on six continents, and have been taught to over two million people.

The ideas in this book are explained in greater detail in *Extreme Spirituality: Radical Approaches to Awakening* by Tolly Burkan, published by Council Oak Books. This popular book can be ordered through your favorite bookstore or at www.counciloakbooks.com.

For information about Tolly's seminars, phone 209.928.1100 or go to *www.tollyburkan.com*.

About the Press

Council Oak Books takes its name from a great oak tree that still grows in the center of our home city. Here the Locapoka Creek Indians established their tribal meeting place and rekindled their ceremonial fire after their long journey west over the Trail of Tears.

Since Council Oak's founding in 1984, the circle around that sacred fire has expanded slowly with each season, like the widening rings of the ancient oak itself. At Council Oak, as in the quiet shadow of the tree, is a meeting place for the sharing of knowledge.

Though rooted in the center of the North American continent, we publish books from people and places all over the world—books that, like this one, cross cultural lines to bring together ancient traditions in new ways. Drawing from history, we publish for the future, presenting books that are destined to become "classics," as they break new ground and point the way to a better, more peaceful world.

To request a complete catalog of Council Oak Books, see *www.counciloakbooks.com*.